Famous Explorers

Vasco da Gama

Tanya Larkin

The Rosen Publishing Group's
PowerKids Press™
New York

For Antoine

Published in 2001 by The Rosen Publishing Group, Inc.
29 East 21st Street, New York, NY 10010

Photo Credits: Cover and title page, pp. 2, 3, 4, 7, 8, 11, 14, 15, 19 © Granger Collection; pp. 2, 3, 7, 12, 16, 20 © SuperStock; pp. 2, 20 © Art Resource.

First Edition

Book Design: Maria E. Melendez and Felicity Erwin

Larkin, Tanya.
   Vasco da Gama / by Tanya Larkin.
      p. cm. — (Famous explorers)
   Summary: A biography of the Portuguese explorer who opened up the lands to the east of Europe by discovering a waterway to India.
   ISBN 0-8239-5555-9
   1. Gama, Vasco da, 1469–1524—Juvenile literature. 2. Explorers—Portugal—Juvenile literature. 3. Discoveries in geography—Juvenile literature.. [1. Gama, Vasco da, 1469–1524. 2. Explorers. 3. Discoveries in geography.] I. Title. II. Series.

G286.G2 L27 2000
946.9'02—dc21
[B]   99-054201

Manufactured in the United States of America

Contents

Growing Up in Portugal

Vasco da Gama was born in the mid-1400s in Portugal. This was during the Age of Exploration, which lasted from the 1200s to the 1600s. At that time, European countries raced to claim land and to trade goods for **exotic** riches. They went to the places we now call India, China, and Japan. Prince Henry the Navigator of Portugal was da Gama's hero. Prince Henry was called "the Navigator" because he planned many sea voyages. He ordered his explorers to sail to unknown places. By the time Vasco da Gama was born, Portugal had the best navigators and mapmakers in Europe.

Da Gama's hometown bordered the Atlantic Ocean. It was protected by a fortress made of thick, white walls. Da Gama decided to become a sailor even though his father had been a soldier.

Prince Henry the Navigator (left) was the hero of
Vasco da Gama (right).

Chosen by Kings

When Vasco da Gama was a boy, he studied mathematics and navigation. This helped prepare him for his adventures at sea. When he was 15, da Gama went on short trading voyages to Africa. On these trips, he became a good leader and sailor. He could steer his ship by looking at the stars. King John II of Portugal asked da Gama to fight French **pirates**. The pirates had attacked Portuguese trading ships. King John II wanted **revenge**. Da Gama easily captured the pirate ships.

Manuel I, the Portuguese king after John II, heard about da Gama and the pirates. He gave da Gama an even harder job. Da Gama was to find a water route around Africa to India. This would help Portugal in the race to claim land and riches.

King John II asked Vasco da Gama to stop the French pirate ships from robbing Portuguese trading ships.

Plans and Preparations

Portuguese royalty and **merchants** wanted to trade cheap items like caps and bells for expensive Indian spices and silk. They also hoped to spread Christianity. King Manuel I gave da Gama ships to sail to India. The *Sao Rafael* and *Sao Gabriel* each weighed 120 **tons** (109 tonnes). The *Berrio* was a small ship that could sail through the water easily. The *Sao Maria* was a **storeship** weighing 200 tons (181 tonnes). This ship carried stone columns called *padrões*. They were used to mark the land the sailors claimed for the Portuguese king. Da Gama brought people who spoke African languages and others who spoke **Arabic**, the **Muslim** language. He also brought Portuguese prisoners that he promised to free at the end of the voyage.

Vasco da Gama bids farewell to King Manuel I as he leaves for India.

The Tip of Africa

It took da Gama's **fleet** almost 100 days to reach the tip of Africa. There they were met by peaceful Africans called Hottentots. The Hottentots traded animal skins and ivory for the Europeans' caps and bells. Da Gama recognized the *padrão* that an earlier explorer, Bartholomeu Dias, had stuck into the ground. Da Gama was eager to sail past Dias's *padrão* up the coast of Africa toward India. He wanted to make King Manuel I happy by sailing farther than any other European ever had.

Within a few months, many sailors in da Gama's crew were sick. They did not eat enough fresh fruit and vegetables to stay healthy. Their skin turned yellow, their teeth rotted, and their arms and legs swelled up. Some of the crew even died.

Da Gama reached India by sailing around the bottom of Africa.

QUINTO CENTENÁRIO DO NASCIMENTO DE
VASCO DA GAMA
1469 1969
LISBOA
ASIA
ARABIA
AFRICA
INDIA
SANTIAGO
MARE ATLANTICU
LINEA EQUINOCIAL
MELINDE
MARE INDICU
BRASIL
SOFALA
3$50
PORTUGAL

12

The Portuguese Face the Muslims

Da Gama needed fresh food and water for his crew. He also needed a navigator to show him the way to India. Da Gama sailed into the **harbor** of what is now called Mozambique. He knew he had come upon a famous Muslim trading post. The Muslims had set up trading posts on the eastern coast of Africa to trade with people along the Indian Ocean. The Muslims did not trust the Christians. They knew the Christians wanted to take over their business. The **sultan** of Mozambique promised to trade two navigators for some of da Gama's gold. The sultan gave da Gama only one navigator. Da Gama became angry. The sultan refused to give da Gama's men fresh water, so da Gama fired his rock-throwing cannons, called **bombards**, into the town. He took the navigators as prisoners when he left.

Muslim merchants discuss the buying and selling of goods at a trading post.

In Search of a Navigator

Da Gama beat the Muslim navigators. They would not show him the way to India. At the next stop, Mombasa, the navigators ran off. They told other Muslims how badly the Christians had treated them. The Muslims wanted to take revenge on da Gama. They were angry that he was in their part of the world. Trading had made the Muslims rich. If da Gama began trading with India, the Muslims would lose their wealth. The Muslims in Mombasa tried to cut the sails of da Gama's ships. When the ship alarm rang, the Muslims fled. Da Gama took more prisoners, but none of them knew how to navigate. They told da Gama that there were navigators in Malindi.

Mapmakers used information that explorers gave them to draw maps of Africa.

AFRICAM
GRAECI
LIBYAM APP:

AFRI
CAE TA
BVLA
NOVA.

EDITA ANT:
VERPIAE
1570.

15

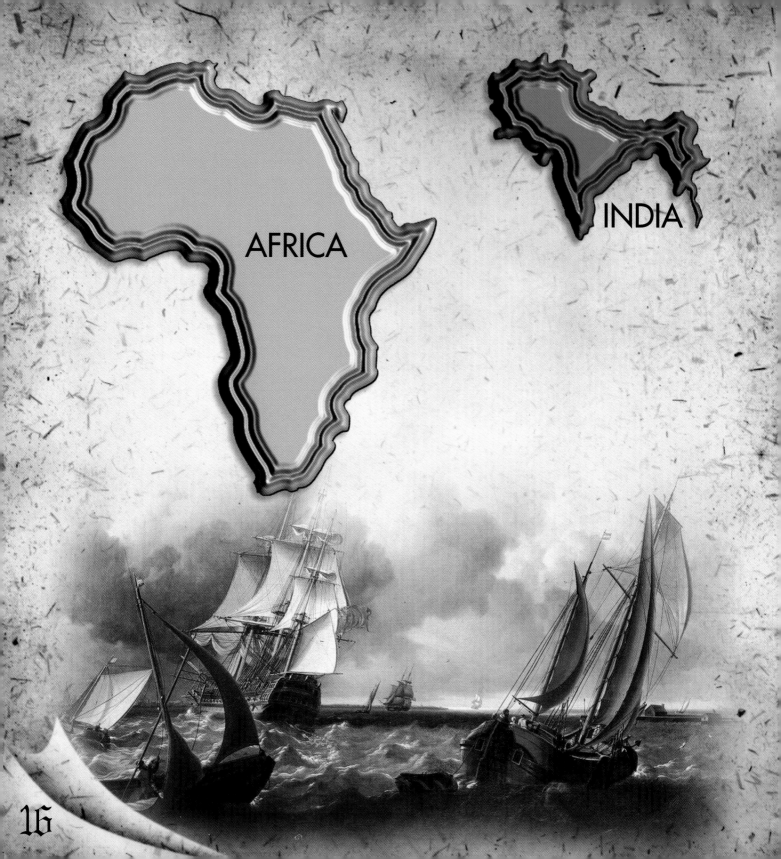

AFRICA

INDIA

Muslim Friends in Malindi

Da Gama sailed to the nearby port of Malindi. Luckily, the sultan of Malindi was friendly. The sultan knew that da Gama had guns and he would get killed if he tried to fight with da Gama. The sultan of Malindi was an enemy of the sultans in Mozambique and Mombasa. He wanted a powerful **ally** like da Gama to help him fight the other sultans. The sultan of Malindi offered da Gama his best navigator, Ibn Majid. Majid was a famous mathematician and sailor. He called himself "the Lion of the Sea in Fury." He knew how to use the winds of the **monsoons** that blew from Africa to India to sail more quickly and easily. Majid led da Gama straight to Calicut, India. On May 20, 1498, da Gama set up a *padrão* to prove he had reached India.

Ships that sailed to India sometimes ran into stormy weather. It was especially important to have a good navigator.

Da Gama Meets the Zamorin

When da Gama reached India, he met the ruler of Calicut, called the Zamorin. The Zamorin was not Muslim or Christian. He was **Hindu**, like most people from India. Da Gama asked the Zamorin to trade Indian spices and silks for cheap European bells and mirrors. The Zamorin was insulted. He wanted more expensive goods from Portugal, such as gold, silver, and scarlet cloth.

Calicut's Muslim merchants did not want the Zamorin to trade with da Gama. They wanted all of the Zamorin's business for themselves. The merchants tried to turn the Zamorin against da Gama. Da Gama was not able to make a trade agreement. Still, da Gama was proud to have found a **waterway** from Europe to India.

Vasco da Gama wanted the Zamorin of Calicut to trade with the Portuguese and not with the Muslims. The Zamorin refused. This tapestry, or woven hanging, shows da Gama at Calicut.

Fighting the Muslims

After a stormy voyage, da Gama returned to Portugal on September 9, 1499. He was treated like a hero. King Manuel I called him "Admiral of the India Seas." After a few years, da Gama received news that Muslim merchants had killed Portuguese people in India. They had also blocked trading by the Portuguese. Da Gama wanted to return to India. He planned to get revenge on the Muslims who were hurting Portuguese people and Portuguese trade. On his previous voyage to India, he had learned that the peaceful way of trading did not work with the Muslims. This time he decided to get his way by using **force**. Da Gama waited near Calicut. In a few days, he was able to destroy a passing Muslim trading ship.

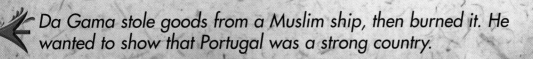

Da Gama stole goods from a Muslim ship, then burned it. He wanted to show that Portugal was a strong country.

The "Vasco da Gama Age"

Da Gama started a violent way of trading. For many years after, European leaders forced other countries to trade with them by using guns. Da Gama went back to India as **viceroy**. He died in 1524, soon after he arrived. He would be remembered for finding a waterway to India. The Portuguese were able to build more trading colonies in India. They became very wealthy.

Da Gama's Timeline

Mid-1400s–Da Gama is born in Sines, Portugal.

1497–Da Gama makes his first voyage to India.

1499–Da Gama gets a hero's welcome on his return to Portugal.

1524–Da Gama dies in India.

Glossary

ally (AL-ly) A group of people that agrees to help another group of people.

Arabic (AYR-uh-bik) The language that most Muslims speak.

bombards (BOM-bardz) Large cannons that fire rocks.

exotic (ek-ZAH-tik) Something that comes from another country.

fleet (FLEET) Many ships under the command of one person.

force (FORS) The power or strength of something.

harbor (HAR-bor) A protected body of water where ships anchor.

Hindu (HIN-doo) Someone who believes in the Hindu religion (Hinduism), a religion that started in India and is practiced by people all over the world.

merchants (MUR-chints) People who sell things.

monsoons (mon-SOONZ) Strong winds in the Indian Ocean.

Muslim (MUHZ-lim) A person who believes in the Islamic religion.

padrões (puh-DROWS) Stone columns that are stuck in the ground to prove that a particular person has been to that place.

pirates (PY-rits) People who attack and rob ships.

revenge (rih-VENJ) To hurt someone in return for hurting you.

storeship (STOR-ship) A ship that carries supplies for a group of ships.

sultan (SUHL-tan) The ruler of a Muslim country.

tons (TUHNZ) A large unit of weight used to measure cargo.

viceroy (VYS-roy) The person who rules a country acting as a representative for the king or queen.

waterway (WAH-ter-way) A sea route for ships.

Index

Web Sites

Due to the changing nature of Internet links, PowerKids Press has developed an online list of Web sites related to the subject of this book. This site is updated regularly. Please use this link to access the list: www.powerkidslinks.com/famex/vgama/